SIGNALS, POINTS & ASPECTS
CORNWALL'S RAILWAYS REMEMBERED

SIGNALS, POINTS & ASPECTS

CORNWALL'S RAILWAYS REMEMBERED

UNIQUE PHOTOGRAPHS OF CORNWALL'S HISTORIC RAILWAY INFRASTRUCTURE

Written and compiled by Stephen F Heginbotham
with photographs from the Frank Sperritt Collection

First published in Great Britain in 2010

British Library Cataloguing-in-Publication Data
A CIP record for this title is available from the British Library

ISBN 978 0 85704 005 3

HALSGROVE
Halsgrove House,
Ryelands Industrial Estate,
Bagley Road, Wellington, Somerset TA21 9PZ
Tel: 01823 653777   Fax: 01823 216796
email: sales@halsgrove.com

Part of the Halsgrove group of companies
Information on all Halsgrove titles is available at: www.halsgrove.com

Printed and bound by SRP Ltd., Exeter

CONTENTS

An undated picture of the Up Splitting Home (PR50/55) at Par. Found by the author during the refurbishment of the offices at St Blazey (Old Station House) in 1994. The gantry signal(s) still exist. Author's collection

INTRODUCTION

THE IDEA for this book came after the death of the person about whom the book is written.

A collection of previously unseen photographs were found amongst his personal effects by his family and in view of the rarity value of these, I had the idea of publishing them as a lasting memorial to the extraordinary, yet ordinary, man that Frank Sperritt was. Royalties from sales of this book will be donated to charity.

Frank was a gentleman of the railway, a man who had devoted his entire life to his career and hobby, whilst still being a family man. He had integrity and professionalism. He was respected and held in high esteem not only by his colleagues, but

On a bad day in April 2000 Frank Sperritt (right) and 'Arnie' Philp came out to one of the Burngullow points which had failed, probably due to the awful weather. The author had arrived first and managed to manually "pump them over" and got the trains moving again. 'Arnie' is standing with the point handle in his hand. I am so glad I asked them to pose for this photo.
Author's collection

by the various managements he had worked for over the years.

When Frank died in July 2007 after a long battle with cancer, he left a void both at work and at home. Frank was stoical to the end, and probably would be both flattered and amused that someone should write a book about his life working on the railway.

You only meet people like Frank a few times in one's lifetime... if one is lucky.

Frank and another technician installing some pointwork and equipment, prior to the commissioning of the Exeter Resignalling Scheme. Circa 1980.

THE AUTHOR

I WAS BORN in 1951 and raised in Stockport Cheshire and after working for The National Bus Company for many years, I joined British Railways as a Signalman at Furness Vale in Derbyshire, transferring to Lostwithiel, Cornwall in 1992. In 1994, with the creation of Railtrack, I was promoted to Signalling Inspector in Cornwall, joining the Operations Team at St Blazey, where I still work as an

Stephen Heginbotham.

MOM in the Old Station House, which was the one time GWR ticket office for the long defunct St Blazey Station. I have a lifelong interest in all things transport, including many years studying railway accidents and incidents that have lead to the signalling systems and rules we use today.

I have been fortunate to work in an industry which is both my hobby and my career, though I feel that changes in recent years within the industry have fragmented the 'big family' that was once BR. I sit on the Area Council as the Rep for the RMT Union and I am also the Local Rep for West Cornwall. I have been married for thirty-nine years and have one daughter and four grandchildren.

Born in an age of steam, I well remember the transition from steam to diesel and electric, and was fortunate enough to see steam to its demise in August 1968, Stockport (9B) being one of the very last steam sheds. As a child I watched named trains with named locos, thunder past my school, and at weekends or school holidays I watched the Woodhead Electrics at Reddish, the trolleybuses in Manchester, or Pacific's on the West Coast or at Crewe, making the journey there by either steam train or pre-war bus. Once a year there was a family holiday in Blackpool, which meant passing the engine sheds at Preston, and many hours watching the trams both along the promenade or at the depot, where I was allowed to roam freely.

I was a member of the preservation movement for many years from the mid 1960s and was actively involved in helping to save some important vehicles for our heritage.

ACKNOWLEDGEMENTS

I express my special thanks to Maurice Dart who encouraged me to get this project off the ground and for his help in sorting the photographs into some kind of order for me to caption. My thanks also go to Simon Butler of Halsgrove. Special thanks also to the colleagues of the late Frank Sperritt, both active and retired, also to his widow, Pat, and Franks' family.

The credit for all photographs is Frank Sperritt, unless otherwise stated. My thanks and apologies also to other photographers, if any of the photographs are incorrectly credited, or names omitted.

Thanks to Tim Oakes for writing the Foreword.

Thanks to my wife, Julie for her encouragement during this project.

REFERENCE SOURCES

Signalbox Diagrams of the Great Western & Southern Railways Vols 14 & 16. G.A. Pryer, 2002
The Great Western Railway in East Cornwall.   Alan Bennett. Runpast, 1990.
The Great Western Railway in Mid Cornwall.   Alan Bennett. Kingfisher, 1989.
The Great Western Railway in West Cornwall. Alan Bennett. Runpast, 1990.
Branches & Byways – Cornwall. John Vaughan. OPC
The Newquay Branch and Its Branches. John Vaughan. OPC, 2002.
BR Diesel & Electric Locomotive Directory. Colin J. Marsden. OPC, 1993.
BR Combined Volumes 1961, 1962 and 1968. Ian Allen
My own notebooks and files which date back to 1959

FOREWORD

I ARRIVED AT St Blazey Depot, Par, in September 1977, to be greeted with an office and depot that looked like an early Victorian prison. Everything about the place gave the impression that nobody cared about this small outpost of signal engineers in the West Country. Little did I know then that I was to begin a period of my fifty years employment in railway signalling that would prove to be the happiest years of my career.

Frank was an absentee in those first few weeks, as he and his assistant Terry Cocks were working away in Bristol "making a shilling" as Frank told me later. When we finally met, his first words were "have you got a big mortgage boss 'cause we need somebody who is going to be hungry." Frank was always very practical!

Frank had by then already gained some recognition for his skills as an installer, but over the next few years that we worked together, he developed those skills to levels that became recognised nationally. His talents became known far beyond the borders of his beloved Cornwall. He was Cornish through and through and never missed an opportunity to let people know what a wonderful place it was that we lived and worked in.

He had countless offers of promotion to further his career 'up county' and declined many times. He would work anywhere to whet his appetite for more knowledge, but he always had to return to Cornwall.

Between 1977 and 1991 the staff at St Blazey and later Par, were flat out with a programme of renewals that meant long hours and hard work. Some notable achievements in modernising the signalling system in Cornwall took place. This meant new skills were needed, especially for Frank. He set about to teach himself the mysteries of electronics, as he hated not understanding "what was in them little black boxes". I would note days in the mess room when his head would be buried in a text book which eventually would take away all the mystery.

There was no time for the sin in Frank's life, as that would not enhance his thirst for knowledge. As a consequence of this I watched through these busy years, the development of a man who became recognised as the man to have in your team. Forever enthusiastic, knowledgeable, hard working and to top it all 'a smashing chap'. I recall talking to some senior managers who were involved with Frank in the development of The Signalling Maintenance Testing Handbook. They expressed their amazement at his knowledge for a Technician Officer, as he was then, and what value his reality check was when discussing the methods to achieve their aims. This contribution was eventually recognised with the award of his 'Silver Wings' from Intercity.

Work was an important part of his life, but it always took second place to his family life, hence his desire to stay in Cornwall, which he knew they loved as much as he did. He also had strong social values, which he expressed through his desire to assist others in what little time he had outside work hours. For many years he was the Branch Secretary of the NUR at St Blazey and we shared a common bond in that area, but he always was quick to remind me "I never voted Labour in my life". I told him he was entitled to one flaw in his character.

The day I was told by Terry Cocks of Frank's illness and the likely outcome, it hit me hard. The memories of all the times together pitting our wits against the problems we encountered and solved together, made me realise just how lucky we were that they helped make life good, when you look at the overall package as we all travel through life.

As I said at Frank's funeral, not many men are remembered as legends in their own lifetime, but without doubt, this is how Frank was, and will still be remembered by the people who knew him. I count myself lucky to have been one of those people.

Tim Oakes
2010

CHAPTER 1

THE FRANK SPERRITT STORY

FRANK WAS born on the 23 April 1949 at Silverwell near Blackwater in Cornwall. He was interested in the railway from an early age and after attending Truro School from 1961 to 1966 and

A picture of Frank Sperritt when occupying his temporary offices (a container) when the main offices were being refurbished at Par, 2006. Author's collection

gaining four 'O' levels, he joined British Railways as a probationer on 19 September 1966.

Frank went on to pass his City and Guilds in Engineering by attending a day-release course at Camborne College in 1968, and from the following April was graded as Assistant Technician within the S&T (Signal & Telegraph) department of BR at Par.

The following years saw Frank rise through the ranks, acquiring ever more technical expertise, which took him to various locations outside his beloved Cornwall and on to such as the Exeter and Bristol MAS (Multiple Aspect Signalling) re-signalling schemes, and minor schemes within Cornwall. The downside of any modernisation of signalling is, of course, the decommissioning of the old mechanical signalling systems, and Frank was involved in the closure and decommissioning of many original signalboxes, throughout the West Country.

The signalboxes that remain operational still require maintenance and adjustment and Frank and his many colleagues within the S&T department were, and are, fundamental in keeping the equipment operational and safe. This requires a certain knowledge and experience which since Frank's death in July 2007, has been greatly missed by both the operations staff and his fellow technicians.

Most of the existing equipment has been installed, modified or maintained by Frank over his long career in Cornwall signalling, and there were no surprises in any of the locations, which included many equipment rooms (Relay Rooms), line-side location cabinets, on-track equipment or signal-boxes.

Frank was a typical old-fashioned railwayman in every way, being totally dedicated to his job and the railway. Very safety conscious, he was a man who was greatly respected by all who worked with him, being of utmost integrity. He was a man who applied the skills of his job professionally and with pride. His knowledge of the equipment and the area was unsurpassed and his passing still leaves a void of both knowledge and character in his depot at Par, and throughout Cornwall and Devon.

As a member of the Operating Department (now Operations & Customer Services) if I was called out to a signalling problem within the area as the Duty MOM (Mobile Operations Manager) I always knew that when Frank turned up to sort the problem out, what he told me about the problem and how long it would take to fix, was usually accurate. The legacy he leaves behind is that those of his colleagues still working in the team in Cornwall continue to operate to his same high standard, and benefit from that wealth of knowledge passed down from Frank over many years.

CHAPTER 2
THE PRINCIPLES OF
RAILWAY SIGNALLING

TO THE uninitiated, signalling may appear to be quite simple, and in order to dispel this myth, I will spend a little time briefly explaining just how complex railway signalling is, in both old mechanical systems and more modern electronic systems.

Mechanical signalling was born of a need to safely move, control and position trains without them coming into contact with each other, except where there was a need to do so. Early railways used Handsignalmen to control movements using a system of coloured flags at key points such as tunnels, and these 'Handsignallers' were Policemen, which is where the term 'Bobby' comes from when referring to Signal(wo)men, who in the PC correct twenty-first century are collectively and correctly known as Signallers.

This simple system quickly became overwhelmed and accidents became more frequent, thus prompting Parliament to pass various Acts to force the railway companies to invest more money in providing a permanent signalling system based on inventions and patents being developed by infant companies who spotted a market for supplying equipment that could offer some kind of mechanical control.

During the nineteenth century railways grew at a phenomenal rate, and the technology to safely move the trains struggled to keep pace with the rate at which companies were building railways. There

A Copy of the certificates used by the GWR and BR to show that Signalmen and Signalwomen were competent to serve in the appointment of their current position.

The GWR referred to Signalboxes as Signal Cabins, different as ever, but a far more appropriate title.

Author's collection

were some catastrophic accidents and disasters well into the twentieth century and these were all learned from in terms of putting in place modifications to the signalling.

Wherever a human comes into contact with a procedure or system there is always the risk that errors will occur and, in an effort to prevent these, a strict book of rules was developed to run alongside the ever-growing signalling. The rules were different for each company and it was not until after 1923 that a more common approach to applying rules became more uniform throughout Britain. When British Railways was formed in 1948 a common set of rules and signalling was slowly developed. These rules have grown year on year and even today the rules for railway signalling and safety are revised twice yearly.

Cornwall is not unique in Britain in having a mixture of old and new signalling. Semaphore signals of the GWR Lower Quadrant pattern still exist, alongside more modern colour-light electronic signalling. Point-work also is a mixture of old and new with traditional mechanical types and power operated types both found within the county.

There are nine signalboxes still extant in Cornwall all built by the Great Western Railway, the oldest being at Par, built in 1879. Par has 56 levers of which 50 are still used, but at the western end there is a small electronic panel controlling the line from Par to Truro, which is now double line again after earlier rationalisation in the 1980s.

Safety is the backbone of all signalling and there are numerous safety devices inbuilt within each piece of equipment. Railway signalling is designed to be fail-safe, that is, if it fails, it fails in such a position so as to protect the trains, even if that means stopping them. Each piece of equipment relies on another, and only when all the checks and balances have been done, will the equipment work as it should. Signallers pulling on old style levers in their signalboxes, can only make the equipment respond by pulling those levers in a set sequence. This sequence can not be altered, nor tampered with. When this equipment is electronic it still uses the same principles of sequence and checks before allowing movements, even though that may only take seconds or fractions of a second to complete.

A copy of the Certificate of Examination used to show the person was rules competent for the position they had been promoted to. The GWR now refers to the location as merely 'box'. Author's collection

But of course, like all things mechanical or electronic, they occasionally fail, even though railway signalling equipment is both robust in construction and vigorously tested and maintained. When this equipment needs attention the railway calls upon such people as Frank and the teams within the S&T, Permanent Way (track) and sometimes the Operating Department, who with their expertise and knowledge usually repair or replace the equipment or put in place robust temporary measures to keep the trains moving until such times as a permanent repair is put in place.

Signalling equipment, includes points, signals, track-circuits and axle-counters (which show positions of trains), warning systems, level crossing controls including CCTV, signalbox equipment, relays and other associated equipment.

This equipment is maintained to a very high standard and the working tolerances are extremely small. Just a couple of millimetres can be the difference between working or failure. Passenger trains travelling over points in a facing (normal) direction are protected by an additional safeguard of the points being locked either mechanically or electronically, and signals associated with these points are similarly locked.

For a signal to clear after a route is set in a mechanical area, the cable that operates the signal passes through a metal slot on the ground adjacent to each set of points and facing point locks in the route. Only when each slot passes across and through each other slot perfectly, will the signal move to the 'off' proceed position, thus proving the route and ensuring each set of points is properly set for the safe movement of the train. In power operated areas where points and signals are electronically operated, these same checks are done electronically.

The levers in the signalbox can only be operated in a set sequence for each train movement. That is because of mechanical 'interlocking', a system which was developed by the Victorian engineers who devised 'locks' that each slide into their respective places underneath the signalbox as each lever is operated. This system prevents the signaller from pulling the wrong lever.

Signallers (Signalmen and Signalwomen) are highly trained over many months before being allowed to work on their own. They have to learn many hundreds rules applicable to the safe operation of their job, and are continually assessed against a strict standard. Their knowledge is tested against a benchmark at least every three months throughout their career. They progress to bigger and more complicated locations, only by demonstrating they are both capable, and suitable for the position.

MOM's are (or used to be) frequently drawn from the ranks of signallers, giving them the added advantage when thing go wrong or equipment fails, that they know what the signaller is or should be doing. Previously known in the West Country as Signalling Inspectors, they are the supervisors of the 'Operating Department' and have many additional skills at their disposal to keep trains moving during failure, crisis or exceptional circumstance.

The technician within the S&T Dept is the vital link in keeping the system operationally safe, and aside from routine maintenance, the Duty Technician will respond to failure caused by wear and tear, lightning, mishap, power failure or other unforeseen occurrence. They work very closely with the Signaller and Duty MOM, and along with the Permanent Way Dept (track) and other railway agencies; they ensure the railway has minimum disruption, performs at the highest possible level of punctuality whilst operating at the very pinnacle of safety.

Each signalbox had a certificate such as this to show who was the Telegraph Inspector, the Signal Lineman and the Telegraph Lineman for the area covered by that particular signalbox. Author's collection

CHAPTER 3

THE COLLECTION

MUCH HAS already been written about railways within the West Country, and particularly Cornwall and this book does not intend to go over ground already covered elsewhere, but instead, I hope to illustrate how one man contributed to keeping those historic locations in safe and working condition in the late twentieth century and the early part of this century, and to publish some of the collection personally taken by the late Frank Sperritt during his long career on the railway in the West Country.

Signalling technicians are responsible for maintenance and installation of pointwork, point motors, semaphore mechanical signals, colour-light signals, track circuits, axle-counters, electronics, level-crossing equipment, including signalbox controls and CCTV, some telephones, signalbox (and signalling panel) equipment, including block signalling, block bells, indicators, track diagrams, train describers, power supply batteries, signalling mini-panels, track-side cabling, relay rooms, control rooms, hot axle-box detectors, and much more.

So when a technician is called out to a fault, they have to be well versed in all aspects of signalling technical expertise, and carry all this out while complying with rules and regulations, and looking after their own safety and that of their colleagues, whilst working either out on the line-side and with the very sensitive equipment or on the track near to where trains are still running.

The Frank Sperritt collection comprises photographs taken by Frank during his pre-railway service and during his early years as a technician. Though the quality of some is not as good as one would like, I felt it important to include them for the unique qualities they possess. Some of the photographs are not included here because of their technical content perhaps being useful to someone of dubious intent, while other images would only be of interest to technical purists, and this book is aimed at the general reader.

In order to lend some order to the many and varied photos in this collection I have grouped them into branch lines, main line, closed lines and, finally, a miscellaneous section.

1 THE MAIN LINE

Between Saltash and Penzance there were signalboxes located at the following locations. Those in **bold** are still extant at the time of writing. The list does not include rebuilt boxes, or those relocated nearby and those previously built by companies before the GWR, such as the Cornwall Railway.

Saltash	St Austell	Carn Brea Yard
Wearde	Trenance Junction	Carn Brea
St Germans	Trenance Sidings	North Crofty
Trerule	Burngullow	Dolcoath
Menheniot	Grampound Road	**Roskear** Junction
Liskeard	Probus	Camborne
Tremabe	**Truro** East	Gwinear Road East
Doublebois	Truro West	Gwinear Road West
Largin	Penwithers Junction	Hayle
Onslow Siding	Baldhu	**St Erth**
Bodmin Road	Chasewater	Marazion
Lostwithiel	Wheal Busy Siding	Long Rock
Treverrin	Drump Lane	Ponsandane
Par	Redruth	**Penzance**
Par Harbour	Redruth Junction	

A poor quality photograph, but worth including. A D63XX class at Menheniot on a down train in January 1964. Fifty-eight were built by the North British Locomotive Company from 1959 to 1962. They worked throughout the Western Region, but were commonly seen in Devon and Cornwall. Not a great success, having a high failure rate, they usually worked in pairs. Withdrawal commenced in 1967 and all had gone by 1972, with none surviving.

D2129 at Doublebois in January 1964. Built in January 1960 by BR at Swindon, it became 03129 in February 1974 and was withdrawn in December 1981 from Barrow Hill.

Liskeard Signalbox in the 1960s. Still standing to this day and with its frame intact, although some modification to the signalling and method of working took place after St Germans Signalbox closed in the late 1990s. It now works to Plymouth and Lostwithiel with Track-Circuit-Block regulations, though the trains are described to Lostwithiel by the original Block Bell.

PAR

THE RAILWAY at Par has always been a hub of both operations and maintenance, being the point at which the majority of all the china clay passes through to the various destinations eastwards, it is also the junction of the Newquay Branch. It is now the main offices for the S&T (Signal & Telegraph Dept) and has a Permanent Way Depot. Par was earmarked in the late 1980s for the site of the new Signalling Centre for Cornwall, under the planned re-signalling scheme proposed in 1988.

The building of the actual centre took place, but alas the scheme fell short of completion due to lack of funds and the embryonic plan by the then Conservative Government to privatise the railways, which commenced in 1994 with the forming of Railtrack.

The building was put to good use though and remains to this day as the home of the S&T and some Permanent way functions.

Reproduced in a separate chapter are two small examples of how Par would have looked had the scheme gone ahead. There were two proposals, one for a rationalisation of the existing track and one for a more flexible use of the existing layouts.

The only part of the scheme ever to be completed was the removal of Largin Signalbox in 1991 which was replaced by an 'NX' (entrance-exit) mini-panel in Lostwithiel Signalbox. The signal and point numbers allocated at Largin and still used to this day, reflect exactly those that would have been had the resignalling scheme been completed.

Called simply the Cornwall Resignalling Scheme, the plans were dumped in a skip by Railtrack and on finding them I asked the then manager if I could have them for posterity, and he agreed to this.

Both schemes would have seen the 1879 signalbox at Par disappear along with its 56+2 lever-frame, its polished wooden instruments, shiny bells and large diagram. The only signalbox left in Cornwall that once signalled Broad-gauge trains.

Class 50 number 50020 passing the signalbox in 1974. Built by English Electric as D420 in May 1968, it was renumbered in Febuary 1974 and was named 'Revenge' in July 1978. Withdrawn in July 1990 from Laira. Author's collection

GRAMPOUND ROAD

D811 'Daring' departing Grampound Road Station on a down train in the early 1960s. Built in October 1959 by BR at Swindon, she was based at Laira and Newton Abbot, which is from where she was withdrawn in October 1972 after being stored unserviceable since November 1968.

An up train in Grampound Road Station in December 1963.

DMU 51586 entering Grampound Road Station on the down in the early 1960s. Built by BR in Swindon in 1961 as Cross-Counrty units with twin BUT 150 b.h.p. engines and mechanical transmission. The engines were based on modified Leyland bus engines.

Bubble Car W55014 leading a three car DMU set on an up train entering Grampound Road Station circa 1963. These 1958 built Gloucester R.C.& W Co 'Bubble Cars' were extremely successful replacements for the old Great Western railcars and survived in Cornwall well into the 1990s, with some of them going on to further use as Sandite units. Some Pressed Steel versions are still in service to this day.

Two views of Grampound Road Signalbox taken in December 1963. The 1892 box closed on 2.6.1972.

Hall class 4920 'Dunbleton Hall' entering Grampound Road Station on a down van train circa 1963. 4920 was built in 1928 as a product of Collett at Swindon.

The station Buildings on the down side platform at Grampound Road in December 1963.

Warship class diesel D806 'Cambrian' passing through Grampound road on an up train circa 1963. Built June 1959 and withdrawn in November 1972 it was cut up where it was built in Swindon in April 1975.

Warship class D803 'Albion' passing the signalbox at Grampound Road in the early years of the 1960s. Built in March 1959, withdrawn in January 1972 and cut up in the following October.

TRURO

Two views of the Interior of Truro West Box prior to closure on 7.11.1971.

Three views of the temporary signalbox installed during the decommissioning of Truro West Signalbox and the remodelling of Truro track and signalling involving the redesigning of Truro East signalbox. This appears to be nothing more than a 'shed' and one wonders just how much room there was inside, though I am certain that Frank and the S&T team would have made sure the equipment was just as safe and reliable as ever.

Truro west Box and loco shed with a DMU departing for Falmouth on a Sunday in the 1960s.

Intercity DMU W52097 at Truro (undated). Built in 1963 at Swindon with two Leyland 230 b.h.p. engines of a type similar to the 0.680 fitted to coaches and buses. Known as Inter-City units they were four car sets with corridor end connections.

West Country pacific 34002 'Salisbury' at Truro on the Down Cornubian Railtour on 3.5.1964. Reputed to be the last Steam train to ever traverse Cornish metals until the era of preservation, though allegedly not the last steam loco, as that was later, when the 13XX class left Bodmin and the county under its own power.

West Country class 34002 'Salisbury' at Truro on the Up Cornubian railtour on 3.5.1964.

D6321 & D6322 on a relaying train at Blackwater circa 1964. Both built in April 1960 D6321 was withdrawn in August 1968, stored [U] and cut up at J Cashmore at Newport in June 1969. D6322 remained in use until October 1971 and was cut up in Swindon in May 1972.

CHACEWATER

Interior and exterior photographs of Chacewater Signalbox including the lever-frame and block instruments, whilst still operational in November 1965. The box opened in 1912 and closed 12.6.1977 with only a Ground frame remaining, until this was removed in the late 1990s.

Warship class D849 'Superb' at Chacewater on a down train circa 1963. Built by the NBL in May 1961 she lasted in service for exactly ten years, then being stored [U] until cut up in July 1972 at Swindon.

Warship D809 'Champion' entering Chacewater circa 1963. Built in August 1959 by BR at Swindon, she lasted in service until October 1971and was cut up at Swindon in October 1972.

D6321 entering Chacewater on the down circa 1963.

Wheal Busy Engine house with the siding being removed circa 1964. The siding was taken out of use on 24.11.1963 and the signalbox closed on 10.5.1964.

SCORRIER

Whilst this photograph is of a poor quality, it is included for its historical importance. The last Down train to call at Scorrier on 3.10.1964, formed of DMU's W51309 and W51324. Both DMUs were products of Birmingham RCW Co in 1960 for the Western Region dieselisation scheme.

Another poor photograph depicting the last Up train to call at Scorrier on 3.10.1964, formed of DMU's W51304 and W51319. See previous caption for DMU detail.

Warship class D801 'Vanguard' at Scorrier on the up in November 1963. D801 was the first production Warship after the prototype D800 was produced some four months earlier in July 1958. D801 a product of Swindon Works, she lasted in service until June 1968, when she was Stored [U] until August, after which she was withdrawn and stored until cut up in October 1970 at her birthplace.

The Down and Up platforms respectively, at Scorrier in Dec 1963.

CAMBORNE

Six photographs of Camborne Level Crossing, Signals an Signalbox all taken on 16.5.1970, shortly before the new barriers were installed.

Camborne Level crossing barriers being installed on 31.5.1970.

GWINEAR ROAD

D1001 'Western Pathfinder' at Gwinear Road on the Up Limited. Undated. D1001 was the first production 'Western' being produced in Febuary 1962, two months after D1000. Allocated to Laira [83D] and withdrawn from there in October 1976 and cut up at Swindon in the following August.

Three photographs of Gwinear Road Level Crossing Gates taken in October 1965.

Gwinear Road West Signalbox and Lever-frame in October 1965. The box opened on 30.11.1916 and closed on 31.10. 1965 with the level crossing converted to Automatic Half Barriers.

Hymek D7038 passing Gwinear Road on the up in October 1965. Hymeks in D7038 was a product of Beyer Peacock in Manchester in June 1962 and lasted until July 1972, being withdrawn from Bath Road and cut up at Swindon in the following June. Originally withdrawn in January 1972 a shortage of motive power resulted in reinstatement the same month. Not a great success, the one hundred and one Hymeks were both unpopular and non standard and pictures of them in Cornwall are relatively rare, so inclusion of this particular one is a bonus.

PENZANCE

D6304 passing Lock Rock on a Truro to Penzance local service in the early 1960s. She met her end at J. Cashmore, Newport, in December 1968 after just over nine years service.

D6307 and warship D812 'Royal Naval Reserve 1859-1959' on Long rock Shed circa 1963. The class 22 lasted until March 1971 and was cut up in Swindon the following December. D812 was built in November 1959 and was withdrawn in December 1972 from Laira, being cut up at Swindon the following August.

West Country Pacific 34002 'Salisbury' backing out of platform 2 at Penzance on 3.5.1964 after bringing in the Down Cornubian Railtour.

Penzance Station in the 'Rail Blue' era, with a class 50 in the yard.

An HST in platform 3 at Penzance in the 1970s.

Class 50 number 50014 'Warspite' in platform 2 at Penzance in the 1970s. 'Warspite' started life in May 1968 as D414 and was named in May 1978. Renumbered in April 1974 and withdrawn from Laira in December 1987, she was towed to Vic Berry, Leicester and cut up in May 1989.

A view from the road looking down on to 08641, 47500 'Great Western' and 50014 'Warspite' in the 1970s. 08641 started life as D3808 in January 1959 and was used as Penzance shunt loco for many years. 47500 started as D1943 in June 1966 and was renumbered in March 1974. Named in February 1979 this Brush product carried the named previously carried by several other ex Great western locos including Castle Class 7007.

2 **LOOE BRANCH**

The historic line to the beautiful port of Looe in East Cornwall was originally built in the early years of the nineteenth century to transport minerals from the Caradon Mines high up on Bodmin Moor to the canal basin at Moorswater. The line was extended during the middle years of the century and in 1860 a further extension was opened to Looe, which closely followed the original canal. There was still no link with the main line which crossed the Looe line over one-hundred feet above at Moorswater. It was not until 1901 that the link was opened to connect the GWR with the line to Looe, though this meant a reversal at Coombe Junction, a move that still takes place to this day.

Signalboxes existed in the following locations:

Liskeard Branch
Coombe Junction
Looe

The token is exchanged at Coombe Junction as the train from Looe arrives and prior to the train reversing and climbing up the link line to Liskeard in April 1964.

A view of St Keyne Halt (for St Keyne Well) looking towards Coombe in April 1964.

Coombe Junction Signalbox which appears to be partly destroyed by fire and in the process of being demolished. The replacement Ground Frame, which is still in use today, is in the foreground. June 1981. Author's collection

3 FOWEY BRANCH

This chapter of photographs deals with the Fowey Branch. This branch line was opened in two stages, with the first from Lostwithiel in 1869 and this was met at Fowey in 1874 by a line from St Blazey built by the Cornwall Minerals Railway. Primarily for freight, the line carried the bulk of china clay to the Port of Fowey and the line from Lostwithiel still does so to this day.

Signalboxes existed in the following locations:

Carne Point
Fowey
Pinnock Tunnel
Par Bridge

A single unit 'Bubble Car' W55018 circa 1964 at Fowey Station having arrived from Lostwithiel. These Bubble Cars took over from the steam Railmotor trains and worked the branch until the passenger service was withdrawn. W55018 was a product of Gloucester RC & W Co in 1958. It had two 150 b.h.p. AEC engines and was transferred to the Midland Region as M55018 circa 1968.

Two views of W55016 at Fowey looking towards St Blazey in September 1964. The Fowey Branch follows the River Fowey from Lostwithiel to Fowey, but the Freight line now ends at the Stop Board at Carne Point. Beyond this the docks are the responsibility of Imerys. Occasional passenger specials have traversed this beautiful line since the passenger service was withdrawn. W55016 is another GRC & W Co AEC engined, Western Region Bubble Car.

A view along the Fowey Jetties towards Lostwithiel in September 1964. The export of china clay from Cornwall is principally done from this port.

A view of Lostwithiel Station circa 1964, with W55031 waiting to depart for Fowey. The tracks at Lostwithiel have altered very little over the ensuing years, except that very little traffic uses the yard now, and the up side yard and buildings are now home to luxury apartments. W55031 (class 122) was built in 1960 by Pressed Steel Co with Leyland engines and differed very little externally from the class 121 except for four character head code boxes on the roof.

4 NEWQUAY BRANCH

The Newquay Branch is another line steeped in history. It is formed of an amalgam of several lines and companies and now forms the link to Newquay from Par via St Blazey and the beautiful Luxulyan Valley, through the clay producing areas of Bugle, to Roche and then over the Goss Moor to St Columb and then on to Quintrell Downs, then past the long closed triangular junction at Tolcarn (Trenance), where the line met the Line from Chacewater. From here just a few hundred yards brought the traveller to Newquay Station, which itself is just a few yards from the Atlantic Ocean. Originally a further line traversed the town centre and down a rope worked incline to the harbour. The line still carries passengers between Par and Newquay, but between Bugle (Goonbarrow Junction) the line also carries minerals (china clay) to the main line at Par and then forward to Lostwithiel where it reverses and takes the Fowey Branch. During the summer timetable Up and Down trains still cross at Goonbarrow and St Blazey, including long distance HST sets, some of which are hired in from other companies, so liveries more familiar with other parts of the network frequently appear at Newquay.

Between Lostwithiel, Fowey, St Blazey, Goonbarrow, Trenance, Newquay, Chacewater, St Dennis and Burngullow there was a myriad of branches, each with a signalbox somewhere along its route.

Some of them are listed below:

St Blazey Junction	Roche	Tolcarn Junction
Middleway Crossing	Tregoss Moor	Newquay
St Blazey Bridge	St. Dennis Junction	Shepherds
Luxulyan	Kernick	Perranporth
Goonbarrow Junction	Drinnick Mill	St Agnes
Bugle	St Columb Road	Chasewater

Newquay Signalbox when still operational. It was on closed on 11.10.1987 after which it stood empty until vandals burnt it to the ground about ten years later.

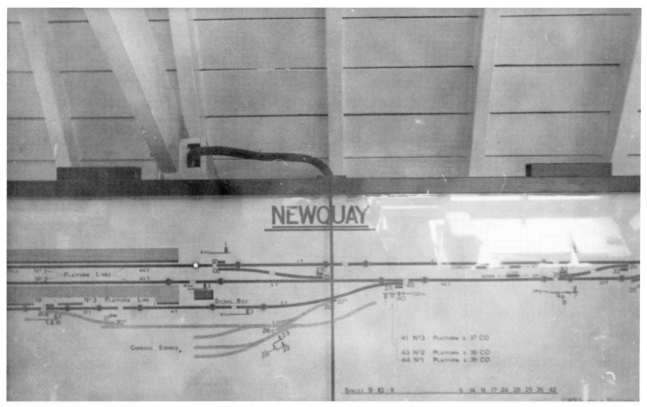

Newquay Signalbox diagram shortly before closure.

A DMU at Newquay waiting for departure on a train for Chacewater, via Shepherds, Perranporth and St Agnes circa 1965.

Newquay Signalbox lever-frame in October 1965.

Newquay Down Loop Inner Home Signal October 1965.

Newquay Down Loop Facing point Lock (F.P.L.) October 1965.

(Previous page and above) St Dennis Junction Signalbox Circa 1965. This box controlled movements to and from St Columb, Retew, Drinnick Mill, and Tregoss. No longer a junction, the new A30 Indian Queens bypass passes over just about where the box once stood.

St Dennis Junction circa 1965, looking towards the signalbox through the old A30 road bridge. The platform was not for passengers and the water tank provided the column outside the box. Only the road bridge and a single track remain.

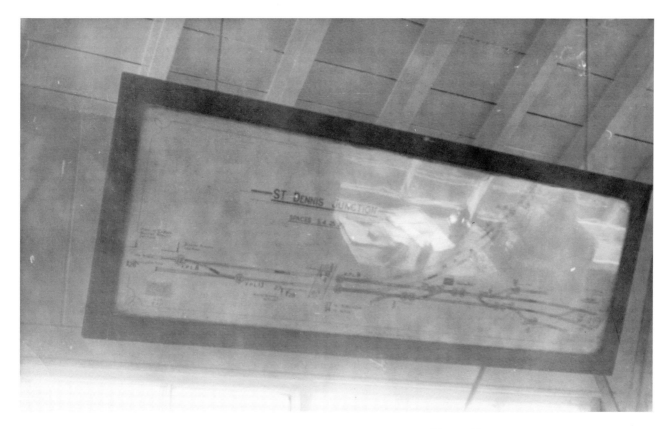

St Dennis Junction Signalbox Diagram circa 1965.

St Dennis Junction Signalbox to Newquay, Tyers Token
instrument circa 1965.

St Dennis Junction to Drinnick Mill Tyers Token instrument circa 1965.

HST set traversing Goss moor ex Newquay in the 1990s. Courtesy Laurie James

ST BLAZEY DEPOT

D6320 and D6323 on St Blazey Shed in pre-yellow warning panel days. D6320 was built in March 1960 by NBL and withdrawn and stored [U] in March 1971 until cut up at Swindon the following June. D6323 was built one month later and stored [U] in April 1971 until cut up in Swindon the following August.

Class 37 37521 passes the Up Inner Home signal for St Blazey approaching Middlway Level-Crossing on 6.5.1994. 37521 started life as D6817 in March 1963. Renumbered 37117 in February 1974 it was renumbered again to its final number in April 1988. Originally allocated to Darnall (41A) it was a 'clay loco' for many years at St Blazey.

Two views of St Blazey Roundhouse with 03, D8XX, D63XX classes and DMU Bubble Car on 5 September 1965.

5 FALMOUTH BRANCH

The branch line from Truro to Falmouth has recently enjoyed a renaissance with the commissioning of the new Penryn Loop. This means that a 30 minute service has been reinstated on this popular and well used line.

Originally envisaged as the main-line for Cornwall, it was opened on 24.8.1863 and constructed for use as a double line, though never laid as such. The Falmouth line and its associated stations at Perranwell, Penryn, Penmere, The Dell (Falmouth Town) and Falmouth (Docks) encapsulate the typical Cornish branch line. Falmouth Town was constructed using parts recovered from Perranporth Beach Halt after 1963.

Signalboxes existed in the following locations:

Perranwell
Penryn
Falmouth

Perranwell Station box diagram circa 1965. The Signalbox closed on 18.4.1966.

D6321 entering Perranwell Goods Loop circa 1965. This view is taken towards Falmouth.

The unusual signalbox at Perranwell which straddled the line into the goods yard circa 1965.

More pictures of the signalbox at Perranwell.

Inside Perranwell Signalbox circa 1965.

Perranwell Station buildings on the down side circa 1965.

Perranwell Station buildings on the up side circa 1965.

Whilst of a poor quality, a rare photo and worth including. Falmouth Station Signalbox Diagram circa 1965.

Falmouth Signalbox circa 1965. It closed on 27.02.1966.

Falmouth box lever-frame circa 1965.

ST IVES

Only one signalbox existed during the GWR era and into BR, and that was St Ives.

Only one photo of St Ives circa 1965 was found in the collection and it is included here. Built as a Broad Gauge box it was one of the very last to be constructed, and dates from pre-1884. Closed on 8.9.1963 and reduced to Ground-Frame status, until full closure on 10.3.1965.

DMU L842 comprising 53314 and 53327 about to stop at St Erth signalbox to collect the Single-Line Train Staff for the branch. The train had come from Penzance. 5.5.1994. Author's collection

6 CLOSED BRANCH LINES

There were many other branch lines in the West Country before the rationalisation of the 1960s much of which came from The Beeching Report. The Line from Bodmin Parkway (Bodmin Road) to Bodmin General and Wadebridge, Padstow, Wenford Bridge, Bodmin North (LSWR & Southern Railway) and from Wadebridge through St Kew, Delabole, Camelford and onward to Exeter, survives in part from Bodmin Parkway to Bodmin General and up to Boscarne, operated by The Bodmin and Wenford Railway as a preserved tourist railway. The Helston Branch from Gwinear Road to Helston via Nancegollan has been closed since 18.10.1964 but there are moves to reopen part of the branch in the future as a preserved railway.

A signalbox (now rebuilt) existed at Bodmin General Station. Boxes also existed along the Southern sections of the line to Padstow and along the North Cornwall Line.

BODMIN & SOUTHERN LINES

View approaching Bodmin North Station in January 1964.

2-6-2T 41295 at Bodmin
North station on a passenger
train in January 1964.
Introduced in 1946 by Ivatt,
the 130 locos of this type
found their way on to
Southern metals during
the early 1960s.

Bodmin North Signalbox in January 1964.

Token exchange at Boscarne Junction Signalbox in January 1964.

Two views of 0-6-0PT 1368 at Wadebridge in January 1964. Introduced in 1934, this particular loco was a replacement on the former B & W railway when the veteran ex LSWR 0298 class Beattie well tanks were withdrawn.

N class 2-6-0- 31856 at Wadebridge in January 1964. The 'N' class were introduced in 1917 by Maunsell and taken into Southern stock at the grouping.

N class 2-6-0 31812 at Padstow Quay in January 1964.

Padstow Station in January 1964. The local service from Bodmin survived for three more years.

A DMU at the buffers in Bude in September 1965.

Tamar Road bridge and Royal Albert Bridge from the cab of a DMU passing Ernesettle circa 1964.

Two views of Bude Station Area taken in September 1965.

ST AGNES

St Agnes Signalbox lever-frame circa 1963. The box closed on 4.2.1963 when the line closed completely.

HELSTON BRANCH

Signalboxes existed at the following locations:

Nancegollen
Helston

A very old gantry signal and associated levers (17 and 20 levers after Jan 1958.) at Helston. Picture undated but after closure of the line.

Some views of
Helston Station
taken in April 1965.

Two views of Helston signalbox, date unknown. The box and branch closed on 8.10.1964.

Views of Helston Station, Goods Shed and Signalbox taken after closure in April 1965.

A view from inside Helston Loco Shed, April 1965.

Truthall Platform, between Nancegollan and Helston, April 1965.

Two more views of Truthall Platform, April 1965.

Two views of Nancegollen
Signalbox, date unknown.
Closed on 8.10.1964.

Another view of Nancegollen Signalbox. Date unknown.

Nancegollan Station after closure. May 1965.

Nancegollan Station. May 1965.

Praze Ground Frame box. Date unknown.

Praze Station after closure. May 1965.

7 **DEVON MISCELLANY**

Inside the relay room at Exeter Middle Signalbox, during the preparation for decommissioning prior to the opening of Exeter Panel Signalbox. Undated.

A class 47 approaching Red Cow Crossing on a down train. Undated.

A view of the frame in Exeter Middle Signalbox before decommissioning. Undated.

Two views of Exeter Middle Signalbox and Red Cow Crossing during the modernisation of the signalling and commisioning of the Panel. Undated.

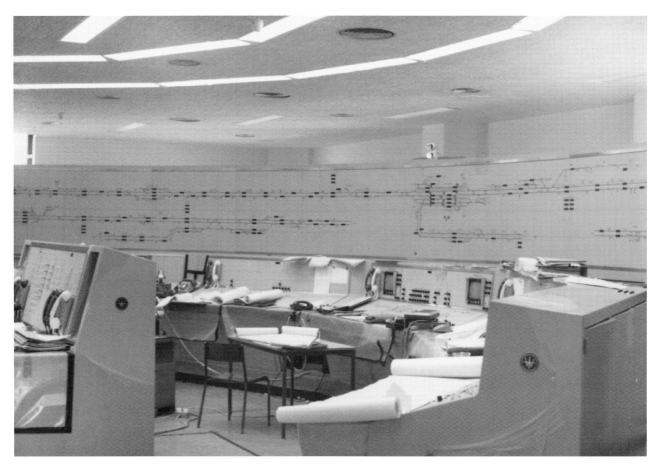

Three views of Exeter Panel Signalling Centre during the commissioning process. Undated.

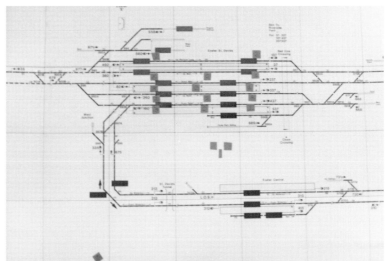

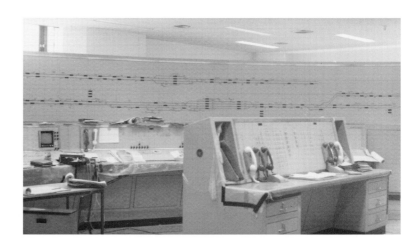

A Warship D8XX, an 08 Shunter and a Western inside Laira Diesel Depot. September 1965.

D1045 'Western Viscount' and two Warship D8XX in Laira Diesel Depot maintenance shed in September 1965. D1045 was built by BR at Crewe in November 1962 and was withdrawn from Laira in December 1974 and cut up the following August in Swindon.

The interior of Laira Roundhouse Steam Shed in Sept 1965.

Laira Junction Signalbox in the early 1960s.

Two views of Laira Junction Signalbox frame taken in the early 1960s.

Two more views of Laira Junction Signalbox frame taken in the early 1960s.

CHAPTER 4

RECENT HISTORY

HERE IS a small collection of photographs of some more recent times on the railway in Cornwall. As a long serving railwayman, I was always aware that history was in the making every day, and as such carried my camera with me everywhere I went. Being a Mobile Operations Manager I am privileged to have advanced infor-

mation of unusual, uncommon and out of course events. Unfortunately some of the dates have been mislaid and other information I had kept in St Blazey up to 2003 has never been recovered after I returned from secondment to Swindon for ten months in 2004.

All photographs in this section are from the collection of the Author.

For several years the long siding adjacent to the Up Main Line at Burngullow, previously used by the Cornish Kaolin Company and known locally as Methrose, was used to store redundant slurry tanks. They were there so long that they were rusted to the rails. In 1998 they were dragged out although they resisted heavily being removed from their long time resting place. They were tripped down to the old sidings at Drinnick Mill, where they resided for several more years before being scrapped. This was the very last train ever to traverse the junction at Drinnick and use the now truncated track down to the Mill. The shunt move at Drinnick required the loco to traverse a short way down the old line towards 'The Barn'. The class 37 worked flat out dragging them out and up the Branch, which was a sound well worth listening to and sadly no longer a daily occurrence in Cornwall.

47306 'The Sapper' in Truro yard with the empty flats, when in regular use on the container train to and from Falmouth Docks. After the work ceased, the loco appeared occasionally on china clay trains before being stored (serviceable) at St Blazey. It was periodically moved around the depot before falling into disrepair and left alongside the turntable before being transferred to the Bodmin & Wenford railway in 2007.

In 1997 the Royal train was stabled in Par Down Loop overnight prior to the Queen and Prince Philip attending functions in Cornwall the day after. Here, early in the morning prior to departure, I had just delivered all the daily newspapers to the royal party. This duty (collecting all the papers from a local newsagent) always fell to one of the MOMs, there always being two on duty when VIP trains were in the area. These trains and their movements were kept secret and on a need to know basis, never appearing in schedules and carry special headcodes and bell codes, even the signallers were only informed shortly before the train was due to pass. On this particular occasion an early morning clay train from Goonbarrow for Fowey awoke the royal party at around 6am as it powered away along the up line, its English Electric 37 loco working flat out, much to the chagrin of those on board. We never used Par Down Loop for such trains again.

On a morning in 1996 the 'Down Sleepers' failed in St Austell platform after limping through Cornwall. In the days when St Blazey had a fleet of locos and several 'spare men' and when the railway was still run for the benefit of the travelling public, the freight department, recently named Transrail, turned out to the rescue. In a nice touch they turned out 37416 in Mainline livery and after I had overseen the wrong direction movement back on to the failed train, I witnessed the spirited departure for Penzance. A class 37 working hard, especially from a standing start was a sight and sound to remember. I had personally been in the cab of many 37s during emergency working and can vouch for the impressive noise they made.

Whilst this is not a particularly good picture, it is worth including for its historical value. Just to prove the doubters, a class 56, 56078 did work along the mainline of Cornwall in 1996, and resided at St Blazey for a few hours, though I cannot recall whether it was ever attached to any CDAs. The trial was for gauge clearance checks in the hope that some of the then surplus class 56s could be utilised on clay trains or other freight because they could pull much heavier loads than the class 37s. They never reappeared again.

In 1995, after a particularly bad winter, the local manager for Railtrack managed to secure seven redundant Mk I BG coaches for use as wave breakers at Penzance. This was so that the MOM and technicians could operate the points and signalling during times of particularly heavy seas, which disabled the electronics close to the station and signalbox. They were stabled in the 'Sea Sidings' adjacent to the sea wall and where the cycle/footpath is now situated. They did help for a couple of years but local residents and businesses objected to the quickly deteriorating condition of the coaches, which were also becoming a refuge for drug dealers, drug users and other dubious activities. After a campaign to have them removed, in 1997 they were towed to 'Kings Sidings' and broken up by a demolition company, only the builders plates surviving, although some emergency equipment left inside when they were first sited at Penzance was recovered and is still in use today in the MOM response vehicles. New track, points and emergency axle-counters now exist to remove the need for constant attendance in winter months, except in very heaviest of weather.

The immaculately kept and well loved chocolate and cream livered class 117 unit number 117305, at St Ives circa 1994. Shortly after this the centre coach was removed to assist in keeping the aging unit mobile.

60038 in Load Haul livery departing St Blazey in circa 1997 after spending a day or so on shed. Class 60s were banned from the Newquay Branch due to weight and bridge restrictions, though they can now use the line up to Goonbarrow.

In 1996 47732 was named 'Restormel' in a ceremony in the middle of the day at St Austell Station on the down platform. The ceremony was arranged between trains so as not to disrupt the service. After the brief occasion was over, the loco was taken to Burngullow and later returned to St Blazey to take the TPO stock down to Penzance.

66124 and 66125 at St Blazey outside the author's office being shunted prior to inspection in the workshops. They were the first class 66 locos to be delivered to St Blazey and had just been arrived brand new off the boat on 23rd June 1999 and the day after were on clay workings.

(Above and next page) Circa 2000 preserved Warship class loco D821 was renamed 'Cornwall' in a ceremony alongside HMS Cornwall in Falmouth Docks. The loco was the first mainline loco to traverse the dock link line for several years and the move was made extremely slowly although the track had been fettled by the P-Way beforehand. Lunch was later taken on board HMS Cornwall in the Officers' Mess.

37521 was named 'English China Clays' in 1996 at a ceremony in St Blazey Depot following a repaint.

D1015 'Western Champion' at Lostwithiel on 19 May 2005 hauling a clay train by special arrangement with EWS and Network Rail.

D1015 arriving at St Blazey with the special train prior to backing in the yard on 19 May 2005.

A rare visitor to St Blazey on 23 May 2007 was class 37 number 37406.

D1015 'Western Champion' reappeared at St Blazey on 28 October 2006 in connection with a special charter, but this time in the maroon livery.

D6990 (EX- 37290 & 37411) arriving at St Blazey on 30th May 2006 in connection with a special charter.

1953 built Standard Class 4 mogul 76079 pulling away from Lanjeth Crossing on the Parkandillack/Drinnick branch on 30 May 2006. At the rear was D6990 which was giving a bit of assistance up this very steep section of railway.

CLASS 60 Number 60055 'Thomas Barnardo' on St Blazey loco Stabling and fuel road on 25 March 2007. Class 60s occasionally appear at St Blazey usually deputising for a class 66.

CHAPTER 5
THE CORNWALL RESIGNALLING SCHEME

A S MENTIONED in an earlier chapter, there was once a grand plan to re-signal all of Cornwall and the 'Bungalow' at Par was to be the Cornwall Signalling Control Centre.

There were two master schemes, one being a rationalisation of the existing railway and one being a modernisation based on more flexibility of the existing layouts. See Appendix Diagrams (Author's Collection).

Starting at Saltash and working westwards, I will briefly outline how each scheme would have worked out had one of them come to fruition.

In the modernisation scheme Bi-Directional signalling would have been provided throughout Cornwall, including additional signals to provide shorter sections and headways (the time/distance between trains) in places where signalling no longer exists.

———— ❖ ————

The existing signals at Saltash on both Up and Down lines would have been retained but supplemented by additional signals opposite them for bi-directional running over the down line.

At St Germans the situation would have be similar to Saltash with bi-directional signals opposite those already in existence. At Menheniot two new signals, one each for up and down lines would have split the long section to Liskeard. At Liskeard

the East end cross-over would have become facing and fewer signals would have been needed to operate the bi-directional running, although the No-Signalman-Token to Coombe was to be retained.

Doublebois would have become a signal section once again, with signal 1021 controlling down line movements towards Largin. At Largin all the existing signals and points now controlled by the Lostwithiel mini-panel would be as they were when installed in 1991, though additional signals would have been installed for the bi-directional running. 1026 would be directly opposite the present 1028 and 1027 would have been positioned across from the preset 1025, each with their own repeaters.

At Bodmin two new signals for the up and down lines split the section to Lostwithiel, then at Lostwithiel a complete rethink of the signalling arrangements streamlined the moves currently available and would have given greater flexibility within the existing timetable.

At Par, like Lostwithiel, a complete rethink of signal positions would have given huge flexibility of movements, though all existing points would have remained where they are now, though renumbered of course. The Newquay Branch would have been Track-Circuit-Block throughout, though there was no mention of the arrangements at Goonbarrow. At St Austell additional signals would have made use of the Ground Frame cross-over as normal operational use. At Burngullow Junction the signalling reflected the old single line to Probus as there was obviously insufficient money available to reinstate the double track, as is now the case.

Truro was to have the west-end cross-over turned around to become facing to assist in any bi-directional movements. No mention of upgrading the line to Falmouth was made, so how the present new signalling on the branch, especially at Penryn, would have fitted in is not known.

Redruth would have gained bi-directional signals on both lines, though ironically Roskear would have only one bi-directional signal for each direction, which is even less than the present arrangement and the existing ground frame x-over was to be removed.

At Gwinear new signals (bi-directional on the up only) would have made this location a signal section once again. At St Erth the east end cross-over would have been turned to become facing, for bi-directional working. Some rationalisation of the old semaphore signal positions results in less signals but greater flexibility.

In the Penzance area little change was to happen with mainly just signal and point renumbering.

Whilst this scheme was an exciting prospect and I for one would have been very interested in working in either the new Signalling Centre or as the local MOM, the associated optional scheme would have rationalised the layout and flexibility of movements even more than actually happened during the interim years to the present day. The second scheme appeared to be designed for a local service between Plymouth and Penzance, and ironically the layout now used at Largin reflects this scheme exactly.

There is no doubt that eventually the signalling in Cornwall will succumb to a modernisation scheme, though this is unlikely to include a control centre within Cornwall, and is much more likely to be controlled from either Exeter or Bristol. With modern technology the signalling centre could hypothetically be on the moon!

Like Cornwall, Plymouth too is unlikely to survive a modernisation scheme as this (very reliable) panel is already second hand, being recovered from Birmingham Snow Hill before being rebuilt to fit Devon several decades ago. Its technology is out of date and because of its age it would not be practical to modernise it. Even Exeter panel, which Frank Sperritt helped to install in the 1980s is out of date, and would not survive modernisation, though its location and the building may survive to house a new signalling centre, should the need arise.

It is unlikely that any of this will happen during the few years of my railway career that I have left, though I hope that I live long enough to see it happen one day. Whilst it will be sad to see all the old semaphore signalling disappear one day, one should remember that even Mr Brunel himself was a great moderniser, a user of the latest technology and an innovator. He would be pushing hard for his GWR to use the latest equipment available and for his trains to be signalled in the most efficient way possible.

We cannot live in the past and if Cornwall and Devon hope to bring in more business by rail, the present railway, in the hands of Network Rail, will need to modernise its business to reflect this. Eventually a scheme broadly similar to these twenty year old proposals will have to be implemented in Cornwall, to deliver the train service of the future.

How things
might have
looked had the
scheme gone
ahead.
Author's collection

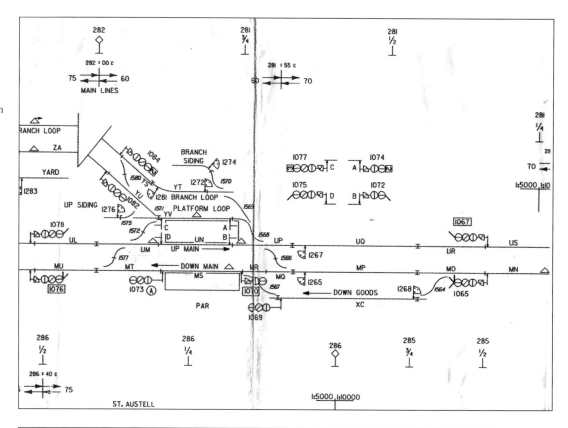

This plan
involved some
rationalisation of
the old layout.
Author's collection

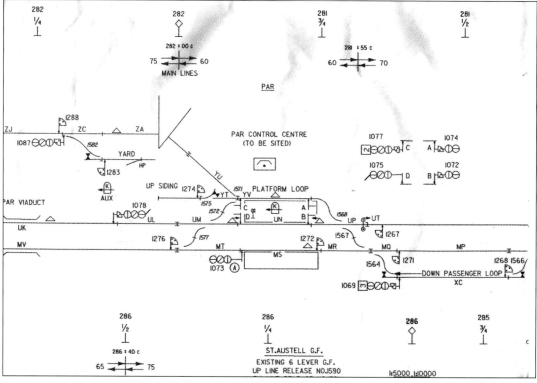

CHAPTER 6
LARGIN SIGNALBOX

LARGIN SIGNALBOX was situated just above Trago Mills Store in the Glynn Valley and controlled the single-line section over the two viaducts at Largin and St Pinnock. A remote and lonely location where it is reputed the signallers used a bicycle to travel the quarter mile or so from the access point to the box. With no running water, a coal fire and chemical toilet, it was about as primitive as one could get. Closed in 1991 after the first

Author's Collection

phase of the subsequently abandoned Re-Signalling Scheme was commissioned in Lostwithiel Signalbox. Largin Signalbox was later demolished. It also reputed to be haunted by an apparition of a young woman who apparently threw herself off Largin Viaduct many moons ago.

Some years ago I was unfortunate to be the Duty MOM late one evening, when I was called to this remote location during a quite violent thunder storm. The lightning had disabled the signalling and point electronics and this meant that the last 'down' train, a three car South-West-Trains 159 unit, was stranded at LL1025 signal, being unable to safely pass over the single line sections across the viaducts.

It is about 600 yards from the access point to the east end points numbered LL1524 and 1525, which required clipping (substantial metal clamps that secure the points in one position) and scotching (large oak wedges). After securing the pointwork I walked up to LL1025 signal where the train was waiting. After some formalities on the telephone with the signaller at Lostwithiel, and the filling in of a couple of forms, I implemented 'Pilotworking', a procedure dating back to the early days of railways in which an appointed person conducts the trains over single-line sections as a human 'token' when the signalling fails.

On reaching the end of the single-line at the west end of Largin, at LL1526 points, I alighted and commenced the long walk back across the mile-long section. It was still thundering, with lightning, blowing hard and raining. It was a perfect setting for a ghost story. As I traipsed along I had a distinct feeling of being both watched and followed. I frequently turned and shone my torch along the shining wet track, with its powerful beam slowly fading due to constant use. The journey past the site of the old Largin Signalbox was spooky to say the least, and as I approached the infamous spot of the reputed spectre sighting I was quite uneasy. It took about 25 minutes to get back to the east end points where I unclipped them and removed the scotches,

before confirming to the Signaller at Lostwithiel that everything was 'back on power' for when the techs arrived to replaced the blown modules during the night.

The journey back to the access point was even worse as the torch had faded almost to candle strength. It reminded me that in the not so distant past my predecessors had nothing more than paraffin lamps and candles to illuminate their way.

AN ODE TO LARGIN

On 16th December Nineteen-Ninety-One

Here are the thoughts of a Signalman,

This is the day Largin signal Box is to close;

Technology and progress I suppose.

What was once a full time job,

Will be done at Lostwithiel with the turn of a knob;

They have installed point motors and locks

To close this small nine-lever box.

No more trains stopping with water and mail,

The end of a Sunday job, to empty the pail;

So Largin Box will no longer be,

Just memories to all and Brian C.

Brian Coad, Signalman

THE DEPARTURE

Never again to wax the floor,

Never again to bolt the door,

Never again to see the sight,

Of a lonely clear silent night

At lovely old Largin in the woods.

It brought on one of my saddest moods

I will truly miss this ramshackle shack,

When I close it on Sunday never to come back.

I will move then to a busier Liskeard

But closing down Largin will still be hard;

It brought me into Cornish Rail

Where the trains deliver the water and the mail.

Sanitation was none too grand,

But the pace was one which I could stand,

So memories will all be good

Of lovely old Largin in the wood.

Perhaps old boxes never die

But time has come to say goodbye.

Frank Blake, Signalman

MY LAST DAY

It is Friday 6th December

A day I shall always remember,

My last day in this old fashioned Box

From where, on one occasion I saw a fox;

Squirrels and birds up in the tree

Has made it a pleasant place to be.

Little mice running on the ground

And different moths flying around,

The robin, blackbirds, jays and tits

All come to feed on little tit-bits.

On to the toilet roof they come

To pick up morsel and crumb.

And in the distance you hear a dog barking

From this old Signal Box at Largin.

Gordon Rosevear, Relief Signalman

COLLECTING FIREWOOD

It was back in Seventy-Seven

That I first came to 'learn' this little bit of heaven,

With Fred Best, Derek Puckey and my namesake "Aubrey"

Who was now to become known as "my Uncle".

With gaps in the Working Timetable,

It has been known for me to disappear

With saw in hand and a "ash or sycamore" in sight

Sometimes a bit late to re-appear.

There was one occasion when old pal 'Ken Wilcocks'

Had the 'London' waiting at Lostwithiel number 'eight',

When I returned the names he called me I will not relate,

Luckily for me the Controller had also had a 'dose of the runs'.

There were times walking down the 'dock' on nights,

Blowing a gale, heavens opening up and not a star in sight,

But once inside the door the warmth and armchair beckons,

The unpleasant weather soon forgotten.

Sunday morning ritual up the 'dock' to read the meter,

Back to the Box and turn up the heater;

Task of the day to empty the bucket

Happy memories now of this little treasure locket.

John Champion, Relief Signalman

TRIBUTE

FOR OVER thirty years Frank and I worked together on some major projects and on faults in the middle of the night. A true S&T Technical Officer, with experience and skill unsurpassed. My railway career would have been a lot less but for him. No praise is high enough for this man and I am proud to say he was also my friend.

Brian Grigg
Par S&T (retired)

L-R Brian Grigg, Frank Sperritt, Paul Gardiner and Matt Jonhson S&T technicians, with PR5/8, and Par Signalbox in the background. The signal (including PR9 behind) is 'off' for a train towards St Blazey and the Newquay branch. *Courtesy Brian Grigg*

A LASTING TRIBUTE TO A GREAT MAN

In 2008 following an email from a colleague, I had an idea about a lasting tribute to honour Frank Sperritt. With some help and funding from the infrastructure side of Network Rail and in particular Dave Gill and his management team I managed to progress this idea.

At that time the new Dobwalls by-pass was under construction and where the realigned A390 road passed over the railway there was a new short tunnel under construction. Looking for a name for this tunnel was easy and tribute to the man it was named 'Sperrit Tunnel'.

The official tunnel plates fixed to the east and west portals.

Formally named on 1 April 2010 at an official ceremony.

Sperritt Tunnel looking east from the old A390 overbridge.

FRANK SPERRITT

1949-2007

OTHER RAILWAY BOOKS FROM HALSGROVE

Halsgrove publish a wide range of railways books covering railway heritage and preserved steam lines. The 'Images' Series based on the Maurice Dart Collection now numbers over twenty titles. To find out more about these and other railways titles visit www.halsgrove.com

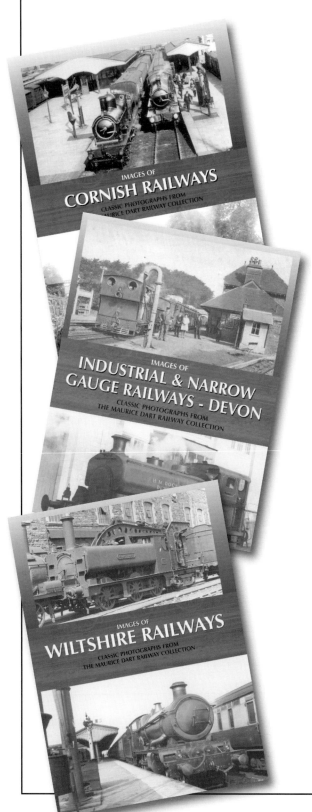

This popular and growing series features photographs from the collection of Maurice Dart, Cornwall-based photographer and authority on Westcountry railways. Here are rare photographs, many of them taken by the author, of important regional locations. Many of these railways have passed into history, although some survive in part as preserved lines which are also included here. Each photograph is accompanied by the author's own text and personal reminiscences.

Now in his eighties, from a boy Maurice Dart has travelled throughout much of Southern Britain armed with a camera, taking photographs of all things railway. His collection, now numbering many thousands of images, has been the source of many small publications and has been used in countless magazines and journals.

NOW AVAILABLE

Images of Cornish Railways
Images of Exeter & East Devon Railways
Images of Bristol, Somerset & Dorset Railways
Images of Wiltshire Railways
Images of Hampshire &Isle of Wight Railways
Images of Industrial & Narrow Gauge Railways – Cornwall
Images of Industrial & Narrow Gauge Railways – Devon
Images of Lancashire & Cheshire Railways
Images of North & Mid Wales and the Border Railways
BR Diesels Volume 1: Classes 24-31, 40-46 and 77

FORTHCOMING

Images of South Wales Railways (West of Cardiff)
Images of Herefordshire, the Severn Counties & Monmouth
Images of East & West Midlands Railways
Images of Derbyshire, Nottinghamshire & Lincolnshire Railways
Images of Yorkshire Railways
Images of Kent, Surrey, Sussex & South London Railways
Images of Bodmin Road to Padstow & Launceston Railways
Images of China Clay Railways (Standard Gauge)
BR Diesels Volume 2